BATTLE AT THE CASTLE

By *Rupert Matthews*

LONDON, NEW YORK,
MELBOURNE, MUNICH, AND DELHI

DK UK
Senior Editor Deborah Lock
Project Art Editor Hoa Luc
Producers, Pre-production
Francesca Wardell, Vikki Nousiainen
Illustrator Mike Phillips

Reading Consultant Shirley Bickler

DK Delhi
Editor Nandini Gupta
Art Editor Jyotsna Julka
DTP Designers Anita Yadav,
Vijay Kandwal
Picture Researcher Deepak Negi
Deputy Managing Editor
Soma B. Chowdhury

First published in Great Britain by
Dorling Kindersley Limited
80 Strand, London, WC2R 0RL

A CIP catalogue record for this book
is available from the British Library
ISBN: 978-1-40935-196-2

Printed and bound in China by South China Printing Company.

The publisher would like to thank the following
for their kind permission to reproduce their photographs:
(Key: a-above; b-below/bottom; c-centre; f-far; l-left; r-right; t-top)
10-11 Dreamstime.com: Konstanttin. **12-13 Dreamstime.com:** Konstanttin.
22-23 Dreamstime.com: Konstanttin. **24-25 Dreamstime.com:** Konstanttin.
32-33 Dreamstime.com: Konstanttin. **32 Dreamstime.com:** Theo Malings
(tl/used 4 times). **33 Dreamstime.com:** Theo Malings (tl/used 4 times).
34-35 Dreamstime.com: Konstanttin. **46-47 Dreamstime.com:** Konstanttin.
48-49 Dreamstime.com: Konstanttin. **49 Dorling Kindersley:** Order of the
Black Prince (t). **58-59 Dreamstime.com:** Konstanttin. **60 Dreamstime.com:**
Theo Malings (tl/used 5 times).
Jacket images: Front: Alamy Images: Tim Gainey;
Dreamstime.com: Fxquadro/Vladimirs Poplavskis

All other images © Dorling Kindersley Limited
For further information see: www.dkimages.com

Discover more at
www.dk.com

CONTENTS

MISSIVE 1

*To Lady Eleanor, daughter of
Sir William Bekes of Horton
in the County of Kent*

Greetings sister,

We have arrived at Oxney Castle. My master, Sir Edmund Perry, is being treated well by Lord Oxney. We have our own room in the West Tower. I even have my very own sack of straw to sleep on.

Our journey was tiring, but enjoyable. Sir Edmund was mounted on his grey horse and I rode the pony and led the two packhorses.

We spied a man in a coracle fishing as we crossed the Great Stour River. Sir Edmund bought four fish for a ha'penny from him and I fried them for our lunch.

As we ate, a barge went by. It carried a pile of large cheeses wrapped in linen. The bargeman told us he would sell the cheeses to a merchant for a groat (four pennies) each. They would then be taken to Rotterdam in Holland in a ship. Sir Edmund said he hoped the French did not attack the ship. The bargeman replied that France and Holland were now at peace.

Sir Edmund said France and England were at war and warned that perhaps the French would attack the cheese. The bargeman sniffed a cheese and joked the cheese was able to fight back. We all laughed.

We stayed the night at a priory. Sir Edmund slept in the Prior's house. I slept in the stable with our horses. It was warm but noisy.

Next day we left at dawn. On our way, we saw a huge pile of wood stacked next to a church. Sir Edmund said the priest would set the wood on fire if the French attacked. Then soldiers would come. Every town near the coast has a war beacon like this.

We arrived at Oxney Castle in the afternoon. It is a small castle with one large stone tower called a keep in the middle. Around the keep is a stone wall with smaller towers. Inside the wall is an area called the bailey. It is mostly grass, but there are several store sheds and workshops. Everyone is very friendly.

Transport Bargains

8 groats Horse and wagon

All-rounder bay horse, 6 years, 16.1 hands, with four-wheeled wagon, arch-shaped canopy, plenty of storage, leather seat, nearly new.

5 groats Fenland barge

Sturdy, 9 m (30 ft) long, cargo capacity 8 tonnes, carries stone and other materials, includes barge-pole, one owner.

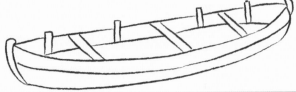

2 groats Handcart

Wooden handcart,
well balanced,
two solid wheels,
smooth steering,
comfortable grip,
excellent condition.

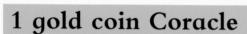

1 gold coin Coracle

Made in Wales, willow, 14 kg (30 lbs), animal-skin
waterproof cover, beautifully crafted for fisherman,
includes paddle.

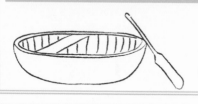

5 pennies Pony

Hard-working Welsh gelding
pony, 5 years, 13.2 hands,
stocky and steady. Comes with
handler: male 17 years, 170 cm
(5 ft 8 in.), healthy and active.

Squire's Daily Tasks

Before dawn

- Wake up! Ugh!

- Collect wood from the storeroom.

- Clear out the ashes from the fireplace and light a new fire.

Dawn

- Wake up Sir Edmund.

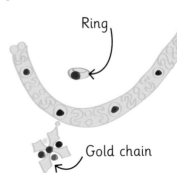

Ring

Gold chain

- Lay out the clothes and jewellery Sir Edmund is to wear.

- Help Sir Edmund get dressed.

Morning

- Fetch whatever equipment Sir Edmund will need.

- Follow Sir Edmund and help him with anything he wants.

Noon

Silver goblet
with red wine

- Stand behind Sir Edmund during dinner. Pour his wine. Hand him a napkin when he needs it.

Fish, carrots and
white bread

Afternoon

- Practise with weapons. Sir Edmund teaches me how to fight and how to ride a horse in battle. My favourite time!

Poleaxe

Evening

- Attend chapel service with Sir Edmund.

- Eat supper.

- Prepare Sir Edmund's clothes and jewellery for tomorrow.

Pottery mug
of beer

- Go to bed exhausted.

Vegetable stew

Brown
bread

13

MISSIVE 2

*To Lady Eleanor, daughter of
Sir William Bekes of Horton
in the County of Kent*

Greetings sister,

It has been three weeks since we arrived at Oxney Castle. We have been very busy as there has been a tournament!

Lord Oxney announced that he would hold a tournament on St. George's Day. He wanted to test the Oxney Array. The Array is made up of the local people who work for the king 40 days each year. Sometimes they repair roads or bridges, but most of the time, they serve in the army.

Sir Edmund was invited to join the contests for the knights.

Days before the tournament, I checked Sir Edmund's armour and weapons carefully. A metal clasp was broken so I went to the blacksmith in his forge in the bailey. I paid him half a silver penny for mending it. I spent all afternoon polishing the armour until it gleamed.

I found a woman to repair Sir Edmund's surcoat and torse. The surcoat is decorated with a golden sword on red cloth, which he wears over his body armour. The pattern is the same as on his shield. The red and gold torse

is a cloth wrapped around
his helmet. Sir Edmund looked
splendid at the tournament.

There was a shooting contest for the archers with a huge prize of 240 silver pennies.

The men-at-arms had to run in armour from the castle to the village and back again.

The women had cake-baking and sewing contests. They had to stitch a scarf with Lord Oxney's badge - a white bear holding a red sword. The winner was given a whole bolt of Lincoln green cloth - enough to make clothes for 25 people!

The contest for the boys who set up tents and dig latrines, was very funny. A pig was let loose in a field. The first boy to catch it could keep it but the pig was covered in grease. That made it very slippery and I laughed so much I cried.

Sir Edmund took part in
the jousting. Two knights have
to charge at each other on their
horses. If one knight knocks
the other off his horse, he wins.
Knights also score points for
hitting the other knight's shield,
helmet or body.

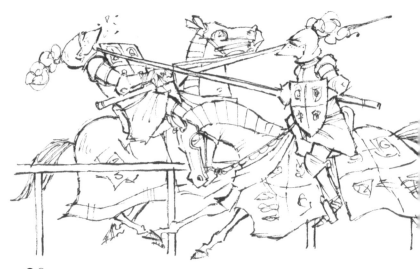

Each knight has a different pattern painted on his shield so that people know who he is. Lord Oxney's son, Sir Henry Oxney, had a white unicorn on a green shield. Sir Giles Black of Hythe had a yellow eagle on a black shield.

Sir Edmund took part in five jousts. He was not knocked off his horse at all! He scored five points, which is good. The jousting was won by Sir Giles Black.

Medieval Fashion Show

"Welcome Lords, Ladies and Peasants! We have a selection of the latest designs on offer made from expensive velvet and satin through to leather and linen. We begin with a range of tough clothes for people working in the fields.

• For all weathers, there is the essential hat to keep rain off and provide shade from the sun.

• Made from wool, outfits come in a variety of popular colours: brown, black, red or green.

• Just for men, we have the long shirt that falls below the waist, plus a selection of brays, or loose linen shorts.

• For protecting feet and hands, choose from the finest leather boots and tough leather mittens.

• Lords, we have long jackets and coats in the finest red cloth.

• Choose from a selection of tight hose.

• Ladies, we have the latest style of fashionable long dresses with long sleeves, a tight bodice and full skirt.

• Not forgetting the essential short underdress made of soft linen.

See more of our fashion range at M & F Stall, Oxney Market on Mondays and Fridays."

23

Design a Coat of Arms

In battle, it is important to recognise people at a distance. Most men wear helmets that cover their faces so every knight and lord has his own coat of arms. The coat of arms allows everyone to recognise him.

To design your own coat of arms, copy the outline of the shield and motto (see opposite page) onto a piece of paper. Then decorate, remembering to follow these rules:

- only use the colours black, white, red, green, yellow, blue or purple.

- the supporter must be an animal or a person. It does not need to be a real animal; make one up if you like.

- the motto must be no more than five words.

- the crest must be an animal.

- the design on the shield can be a shape, an animal, a plant or a mix of all three.

- the mantle must be in the same colours as the shield.

Crest

Mantle

Shield

Supporter

Motto

STRONG AND TRUE

MISSIVE 3

*To Lady Eleanor, daughter of
Sir William Bekes of Horton
in the County of Kent*

In haste sister,

A French army has landed in
Hastings! We received this exciting
news three days ago. However,
many local people are very worried.
Lord Oxney is preparing to fight.
Sir Edmund has been given
command of 50 men from the local
Array. We have so much to do.

At dawn, the French army
ran ashore armed with swords
and axes. They captured the Mayor
of Hastings and made him pay
50 pounds of silver. They said
they would burn the town if
he did not pay.

Lord Oxney issued a Commission of Array. That means that all the Array must come to Oxney Castle, bringing their weapons and armour.

This morning the French burned Iden, which is less than an hour's walk from here!
Sir Edmund told me the French burn a village if the people run away without paying money.

The people from Oxney have been coming to the castle. They are bringing their farm animals, money, grain and farm tools. About 200 people are now camped in the bailey. They have built some wooden sheds to sleep in.

The people believe they will be safe here. They say the stone walls will stop the French soldiers. I hope they are right.

Sir Edmund led his 50 men out of the castle. I accompanied him. We went south and stopped by a ford over the River Rother. The French will have to come across this ford so five scouts were sent riding south to look for them.

This afternoon one scout returned accompanied by the French herald. I led the herald to Oxney Castle to speak to Lord Oxney and it was announced that the siege of Oxney Castle would begin tomorrow.

I send this letter by the last messenger before the siege begins. God bless us all and keep us safe.

War Dialogue

This is the conversation between the French herald (red) and the Earl of Oxney (blue) that I overheard. They followed the etiquette of medieval warfare.

My Lord Oxney, my master Baron de Gilles sends his greetings to you.

The Baron is very kind. I remember we met at the tournament in Bruges two years ago. I trust he and his charming wife, Eloise are well?

Indeed, my lord. They are very well. My master asks about the health of your wife, Lady Mary, and your son, Sir Henry.

They are very well, thank you.

Baron de Gilles remembers you kindly. He is sad that our nations are at war. Even so he would like to visit you here at Oxney Castle.

I would be honoured, but my castle is full at the moment. I have many guests.

How sad. Baron de Gilles says that he would be willing to go away. All he asks is that you pay him 100 pounds of silver. Then he will go back to France.

The Baron makes a kind offer, but I will not pay a man not to visit me.

Then Baron de Gilles will come here. He will enter with his army and kill you all, including you, your wife and your son.

Please tell Baron de Gilles that I will enjoy defeating him here just as I did at the tournament at Bruges. Goodbye, Monsieur.

Dressed in Armour

Every morning I help Sir Edmund put on his armour. This must be done properly so that he can be protected when he fights the French.

First, Sir Edmund puts on his undershirt. This has patches of metal chain mail to cover gaps in the outer armour. Then I strap on his metal leg armour.

Next, the body armour is strapped on. Below the breastplate are loose dangling sections to cover the bottom and lap.

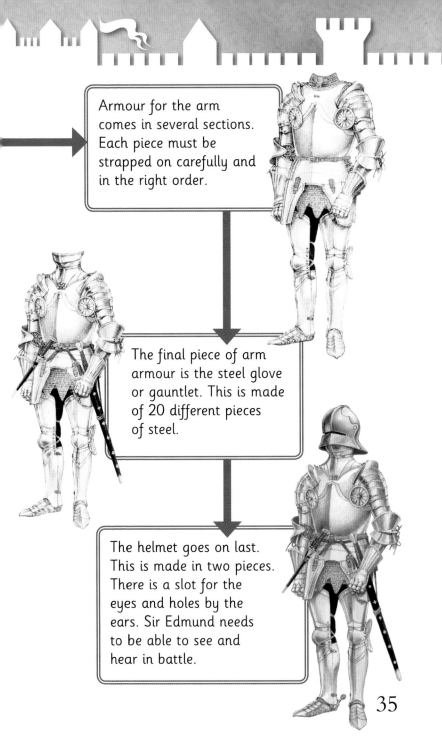

Armour for the arm comes in several sections. Each piece must be strapped on carefully and in the right order.

The final piece of arm armour is the steel glove or gauntlet. This is made of 20 different pieces of steel.

The helmet goes on last. This is made in two pieces. There is a slot for the eyes and holes by the ears. Sir Edmund needs to be able to see and hear in battle.

MISSIVE 4

*To Lady Eleanor, daughter of
Sir William Bekes of Horton
in the County of Kent*

Sister,

We are in great danger. You must
help us. The siege is going badly
for us. Let me explain.

    After the French herald left,
the siege began. The French army
arrived the next morning.
We watched from the castle walls.
We saw knights, crossbowmen,
men-at-arms, men with spears,
men with axes and Baron de Gilles.
The Baron had a coat of arms of
a green dragon on a yellow shield.
Beside him rode a man carrying
a large flag with the green dragon.

The French soldiers set up tents in a field. Baron de Gilles and three other knights rode forward to study the castle. Sir Edmund said they were looking for a weak spot. These French knights came closer. Lord Oxney called for the archer who had won the contest at our tournament.

He told the man to shoot
an arrow at the French knights.
The archer shot his arrow and
it hit the ground just beside
the man with the flag. The horse
reared up and the man dropped
the flag. We all laughed.

For the rest of the day, the French cut down trees. They built a fence right around the castle. French soldiers patrolled along the fence to stop anyone getting in or out of the castle. Our archers tried shooting them, but the fence was too far away.

Next day the French began their attack. The men armed with crossbows came forward. Each man had a large wooden shield carried by a second man. Sir Edmund said the shields are called pavises. The crossbow bolts reached the castle walls. One of our men was hit in the shoulder and he was taken to the doctor. After that we kept down behind the parapet.

On the third day, the French brought up their two siege engines. The ballista shot large wooden bolts at the gate. Every time a bolt hit, the gate shook, but it did not break. The trebuchet threw large rocks that went up high then crashed down. Some landed in the bailey, smashing anything they hit. Several people were killed. One stone hit the keep and made a hole in the roof.

Lord Oxney told Sir Edmund to destroy the siege engines. That night Sir Edmund led his 50 men out of a small gate.

We crept towards the siege engines.
When we got there, we began
piling up bundles of twigs.
Then Sir Edmund told me to light
a fire. The French saw the flames
and attacked.

There was a big fight in the dark. Several men on both sides were killed. We carried our wounded back to the castle. Then we watched as the trebuchet burned, but the ballista was not destroyed.

Next morning, a terrible thing happened. The well ran dry. You know how dry the weather has been. The underground stream beneath the castle has no water in it. We have plenty of food and weapons, but we cannot live without water. You must tell father. Tell him we need an army to help us. I send this message in the hands of a boy who says he can get over the fence. God save us all.

Castle Defences

Bailey
During a siege, local people camp here for safety.

Walls
The stone walls protect the bailey from attack.

Moat
The moat is filled with water to make an attack more difficult.

Gatehouse
The gate is the weakest part of the defences.

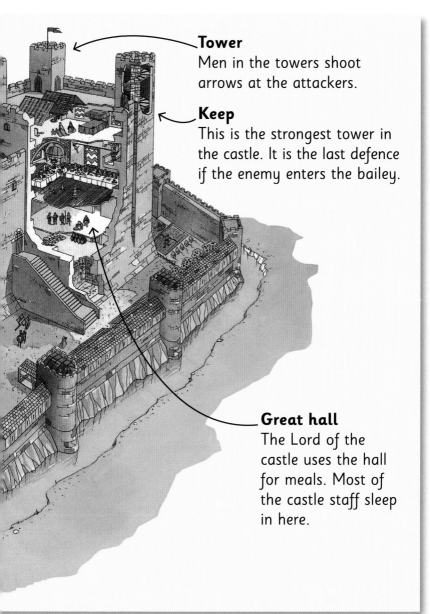

Tower
Men in the towers shoot arrows at the attackers.

Keep
This is the strongest tower in the castle. It is the last defence if the enemy enters the bailey.

Great hall
The Lord of the castle uses the hall for meals. Most of the castle staff sleep in here.

47

Siege Engines

A siege army used some terrifying large weapons to attack over the high stone walls of a castle.

Trebuchet

The trebuchet is like a giant sling. The sling is lowered to the ground.

1. A large rock is put in the sling.

1

2. Next, several men pull down on the ropes as hard as they can, turning the lever arm.

3

2

3. As the lever arm turns, the sling is lifted into the air very quickly. When the sling stops, the stone is thrown up and forwards.

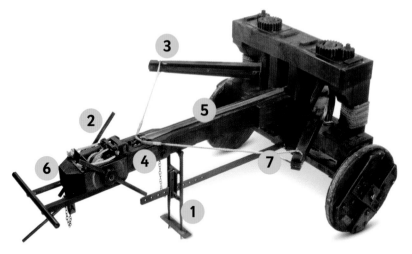

Ballista

The ballista is like a giant bow. It is much smaller than the trebuchet.

1. Once it is wheeled into position, the stand is put in place to keep it still.

2. The windlass is used to wind back the rope.

3. As the rope is pulled back, the arms are pulled back. The arms are connected to coiled sinew (twisted strands).

4. When the rope is back far enough, it is caught on a hook.

5. The missile is loaded. This could be a wooden dart with iron points.

6. When the trigger is pulled, the hook holding the rope drops.

7. As the sinews snap back, they pull the arms straight. The arms yank the rope forwards, firing the missile.

49

MISSIVE 5

*To Lady Eleanor, daughter of
Sir William Bekes of Horton
in the County of Kent*

Greetings sister,

Good news! The siege of Oxney Castle is over. We are safe. Thank you, dear sister, thank you.

At dawn this morning, the lookout shouted for Lord Oxney. We all went up to the walls and saw Baron de Gilles on his horse, shouting orders. The Frenchmen were taking down their tents. They put on their armour and formed up in lines ready for battle.

Far to the north, we saw a great column of smoke from a war beacon.

Then we saw men on horses
on a hill far away to the north.
One of the men waved a flag.
Lord Oxney called his herald and
asked who the horsemen were.
The herald stared. He must have
good eyesight for he said it was a
red flag with something gold on it.

Half an hour later, men on foot came out of the woods. Our herald stood watching the flags and shields. He kept calling out names as he recognised the patterns:

"Sir William Moon."
"Lord Layne."
"Sir Ralph Foxton."

Then everyone started cheering and shouting. The horsemen with the red flag had arrived. The pattern was three gold lions on the red flag. It was the Royal Banner. The King of England himself was here.

The English army drew up facing the French with the knights in the middle and the archers on either side. The men on horseback were behind them. Then the battle began.

The English archers shot their arrows at the French. The French charged forwards. There was a loud whistling noise as thousands of arrows flew through the air. All the French wore armour, but several were killed or wounded. The English knights were singing.

There was a loud crash as the two armies met. We heard the noise of swords hitting shields.

54

Men were shouting in anger or
screaming in pain.

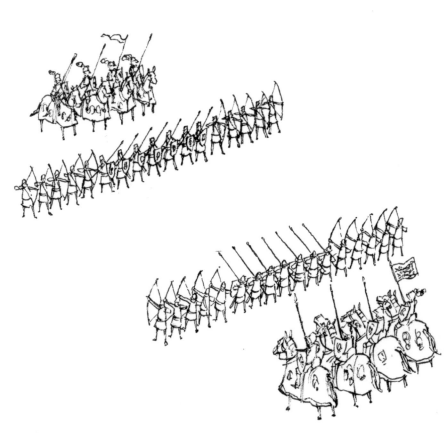

Suddenly, the French turned and fled. The English horsemen gave chase, killing some and taking others prisoner. Baron de Gilles escaped back to his ship. He forgot to take his chest of silver so the Mayor of Hastings got his money back!

Lord Oxney says everyone who was in the castle for the siege will get a new set of clothes – even shoes and underwear.
He is paying for it all. I am getting a suit of brown woollen cloth with brass buttons.

The King is staying here and Lord Oxney is holding a great feast to celebrate defeating the French. I send you an invitation with this missive. Please come. Everyone wants to thank you for getting the message to the King.

Victory Party

An invitation from
Lord and Lady Oxney of Oxney Castle
in the County of Kent.

The presence of
Lady Eleanor, daughter of Sir William Bekes
of Horton in the County of Kent,
is requested.

There will be a Grand Feast to celebrate
the defeat of Baron de Gilles.

58

The Grand Feast will be held
at **Oxney Castle**
on the day of **St. Petroc of Padstow.**

In attendance will be the
**King of England, the Earl of Lincoln
and the Countess of Kent.**

Entertainment by jugglers, minstrels, bards,
tumblers, dancing bears and performing dogs.
Dancing will take place to the music of
the Canterbury Carollers.

Best clothes must be worn.
Weapons must be left at the door.
Servants may be brought. They may
attend the party held in the bailey.

BATTLE AT THE CASTLE QUIZ

 1. What was the animal on Lord Oxney's badge?

 2. Where did the French army land?

 3. What were thrown from a trebuchet?

 4. Who had a red flag with three gold lions?

 5. On what day was the Grand Feast held?

Answers on page 64.

60

GLOSSARY

bolt
medieval unit of measurement about 36.5 metres (40 yds)

coracle
small, round boat

etiquette
how to behave in a conversation

groat
silver coin worth four pennies

ha'penny
coin worth half of a penny

herald
messenger

medieval
time between 500–1500CE

missive
written message or letter

Prior
second-most important monk

siege
army surrounds a castle and attempts to capture it

squire
young boy training to be a knight

surcoat
decorated tunic worn by a knight

Guide for Parents

DK Reads is a three-level interactive reading adventure series for children, developing the habit of reading widely for both pleasure and information. These chapter books have an exciting main narrative interspersed with a range of reading genres to suit your child's reading ability, as required by the National Curriculum. Each book is designed to develop your child's reading skills, fluency, grammar awareness, and comprehension in order to build confidence and engagement when reading.

Ready for a *Starting to Read Alone* book

YOUR CHILD SHOULD

- be able to read most words without needing to stop and break them down into sound parts.
- read smoothly, in phrases and with expression. By this level, your child will be mostly reading silently.
- self-correct when some word or sentence doesn't sound right.

A VALUABLE AND SHARED READING EXPERIENCE

For some children, text reading, particularly non-fiction, requires much effort but adult participation can make this both fun and easier. So here are a few tips on how to use this book with your child.

TIP 1 Check out the contents together before your child begins:

- invite your child to check the blurb, contents page and layout of the book and comment on it.
- ask your child to make predictions about the story.
- chat about the information your child might want to find out.

TIP 2 Encourage fluent and flexible reading:

- support your child to read in fluent, expressive phrases, making full use of punctuation and thinking about the meaning.

- encourage your child to slow down and check information where appropriate.

TIP 3 Indicators that your child is reading for meaning:

- your child will be responding to the text if he/she is self-correcting and varying his/her voice.

- your child will want to chat about what he/she is reading or is eager to turn the page to find out what will happen next.

TIP 4 Praise, share and chat:

- the factual pages tend to be more difficult than the story pages, and are designed to be shared with your child.

- encourage your child to recall specific details after each chapter.

- provide opportunities for your child to pick out interesting words and discuss what they mean.

- discuss how the author captures the reader's interest, or how effective the non-fiction layouts are.

- ask questions about the text. These help to develop comprehension skills and awareness of the language used.

A FEW ADDITIONAL TIPS

- Read to your child regularly to demonstrate fluency, phrasing and expression; to find out or check information; and for sharing enjoyment.

- Encourage your child to reread favourite texts to increase reading confidence and fluency.

- Check that your child is reading a range of different types, such as poems, jokes and following instructions.

Series consultant **Shirley Bickler** is a longtime advocate of carefully crafted, enthralling texts for young readers. Her LIFT initiative for infant teaching was the model for the National Literacy Strategy Literacy Hour, and she is co-author of *Book Bands for Guided Reading* published by Reading Recovery based at the Institute of Education.

INDEX

Answers to the Battle at the Castle Quiz:
1. A white bear; **2.** Hastings; **3.** Large rocks;
4. The King of England; **5.** St. Pedroc of Padstow's Day.